S0-BZS-847

Sarah and Paul
Go to the Seaside

Discover about
The Holy Spirit
and
The Church

Derek Prime

Christian Focus Publications

© Derek Prime
ISBN 1 871 676 347

Published by
Christian Focus Publications Ltd, Geanies House,
Fearn, Ross-shire, IV20 1TW, Scotland
website: http://www.geanies.org.uk/cfp

1st edition 1989
2nd edition 1994
3rd edition 1998

Cover design by Donna Macleod
Cover illustration by Andrew Tudor, Allied Artists

Printed and bound in Great Britain by
Caledonian, Glasgow

CONTENTS

To Anna, Emily, Deborah, Andrew and Paul

1   Making Plans

Sarah MacDonald woke up before her twin brother, Paul. She listened, but couldn't hear a sound, so it wasn't her parents' alarm clock which had woken her up. She crept downstairs to the hall to see what the time was. It was only 6.15 - another three quarters of an hour before the alarm would ring. Sarah was very excited because it was the Friday before school finished for the spring holiday, and her father was going to have time off from work. He had promised to take them to Grandma and Grand-dad's cottage by the sea. In turn, Grandma and Grand-dad had offered to stay in Paul and Sarah's home to look after the cat and the goldfish. Sarah was bursting with ideas of things to do. She decided to wake up Paul and tell him all about them. She tiptoed into his bedroom and whispered in his ear, 'Wake up, Paul!'

'What is it?' answered Paul with a yawn. 'Is it time to get up?'

'No, not yet. Another three quarters of an hour.'

'What did you want to wake me up for then, silly?' replied Paul. 'I'm tired. Go back to bed and leave me alone.' He turned over to his other

side as if to go back to sleep.

'Oh, no you don't, old lazybones,' exclaimed Sarah. 'Our spring holiday begins today and it's time we made our plans.'

The reminder of school finishing for a while made Paul feel a little happier at Sarah's waking him so early.

'So it is. Let's begin to make our plans!' he shouted.

'Shh!' whispered Sarah. 'Mum and Dad are still asleep. Don't make such a noise. Look, I've found Dad's guidebook and it looks as if there are all kinds of interesting things to explore near where we'll be staying. There's a large park, a famous cave and an old church.'

'I hope the weather's all right,' exclaimed Paul.

'Dad said the weather was good this time last year,' replied Sarah. 'Let's write down what we want to do when we get to the cottage.'

* * *

'You look happy, Paul,' commented Mr MacDonald as Paul came leaping down the stairs for breakfast.

'I am,' answered Paul. 'We start our holiday today. Sarah and I've been making a list of all the things we're going to do.'

7

'We're going to put up our tent in the back garden tomorrow if the weather's warm enough,' added Sarah, who had just come down.

'It's good having some days together, isn't it?' said Paul.

Mr MacDonald smiled and nodded. He was looking forward to the time away too.

'Have you remembered what next Sunday is?'

'Whitsunday,' replied Sarah. 'I had to tell my class about it because Mrs Fox knew that I would have a lesson about it in Sunday School.'

'What did you say to your class?' asked her father.

'I said that it's the time in the year when we remember that God sent the Holy Spirit to the disciples as they waited at Jerusalem. I told what happened to the disciples, how they were made very bold and were able to tell others about the Lord Jesus.'

At that moment Mrs MacDonald called out from the kitchen, 'What do you all want this morning for breakfast? Scrambled eggs or eggs and bacon?'

'Eggs and bacon, please,' shouted Paul and Sarah.

Sarah began to put the place mats on the

8

table and Paul counted out the right number of knives and forks.

Paul had been listening to Sarah and he thought of a question he wanted to ask his father.

'Did it come into the world for the first time on Whitsunday?'

'I don't know what you mean,' said Mr MacDonald.

'I mean the Holy Spirit,' explained Paul.

'You're making a mistake then,' replied his father.

'How?'

'Do you know, Sarah?'

She thought for a moment. 'Yes, I think so. Paul said, "Did it come into the world for the first time?" The Holy Spirit isn't it but He.'

Mr MacDonald nodded. 'That's right. You speak of a thing as it. If we were talking about our car, we might say, "It needs to be washed." Or we might say about the phone, "It's ringing." But if we saw a man coming up our path to deliver something, we'd say, "Here he comes" because the delivery man's a person. The Holy Spirit isn't a thing, but He's a Person. When the Lord Jesus spoke about the Holy Spirit, He always called Him "He" and never "it". How would you like to be called "it", Paul?'

'I wouldn't,' retorted Paul.

'You've learned something important then. Remember that the Holy Spirit's a Person and that we may upset Him by our sin, even as you and I may upset one another by doing wrong things.'

'Did He come into the world for the first time that Whitsunday?'

Mr MacDonald was sure that Paul and Sarah ought to be able to answer this question themselves. 'What do you think?'

Paul and Sarah looked at one another and didn't answer. Mr MacDonald decided to help them. 'Can you remember our talking about the Holy Spirit before?'

Sarah remembered first. 'When you explained to us about the Trinity - how there's only one God, but He makes Himself known to us in three Persons.'

'Good,' said Mr MacDonald. 'Now, can you remember the passage in the Bible we looked at where it tells us about God the Father, God the Son and God the Holy Spirit doing something together?'

'Yes, I know,' Paul remembered. 'It was

Jesus' baptism. God the Father spoke from heaven. And then the Holy Spirit came down on Jesus, like a dove.'

Mr MacDonald smiled. 'Yes, that's right. Now you've almost answered your own question.'

'I see,' said Paul. 'The Holy Spirit was here on earth before the first Whitsunday because He was with the Lord Jesus when He was on earth.'

'There's more to it than that,' Mr MacDonald went on. 'The Holy Spirit had a lot to do with the Lord Jesus' coming to live in this world. He made possible the birth of the Lord Jesus without a human father. He helped the Lord Jesus in the wonderful things He did. It was the Holy Spirit too who raised Jesus from the dead.'

'I didn't know He did all those things!' exclaimed Sarah with surprise. 'But did the Holy Spirit ever help ordinary people like us?'

'Yes, He did. He helped, for example, all the people who wrote the Bible. He made them feel they ought to write down God's message to them, and without their knowing sometimes the full meaning of what they wrote, He showed them what to write. He helped them to write about things in the future no one else knew would happen. He let them into some of God's secrets to prepare people for them.'

'I should have remembered that,' Paul said.

By now the smell of eggs and bacon was drifting into the room from the kitchen.

'Mm! Smells good!' murmured Mr MacDonald.

'I've a question too, Dad.' said Sarah.

Mr MacDonald nodded.

'Did the Holy Spirit do anything else before Jesus came?'

'He certainly did,' answered Mr MacDonald. 'He had a lot to do with the creation of the world. The first chapter of the Bible tells us something about that. All the beautiful things you see in the world - the birds, the animals, the trees, the flowers, indeed all the wonders of nature - are things God has made. Whenever you see something wonderful and beautiful like that in the world, you may be sure that it's God's work. Always remember that the Holy Spirit is the third Person of the Trinity.'

'It was rather silly of me to ask if He began His work on that first Whitsunday, wasn't it?'

12

exclaimed Paul.

'No, it wasn't silly at all,' replied Mr MacDonald. 'It's sensible to ask questions. That's how we learn. The Holy Spirit didn't come into the world for the first time on the day of Pentecost, the day many Christians call Whitsunday. But He did come in a new and special way at that time to be with Christians and to live with them. I'm sure we'll hear something about Him at church on Sunday morning.'

At that moment Mrs MacDonald came in with two plates of bacon and eggs. 'Bring the other two plates in, please, Sarah. I suggest you stop talking and eat your breakfast or you'll be late for school at this rate!'

'And I'll be late for my work,' added Mr MacDonald.

13

2 Talk at Sunday Dinner

The next Sunday was a warm day and by the time the MacDonald family were halfway through their dinner Paul was feeling very hot.

'Phew!' he exclaimed, while his mother was cutting up the apple pie. 'I wish we were already by the sea.'

'You won't have to wait long now,' said Mr MacDonald. 'Wasn't it warm in church this morning? I'm glad they opened all the windows.'

'There were lots of people away, weren't there?' commented his wife, as she passed the plates around. 'Sarah, serve the ice cream, please.'

'Quite a few visitors were at church to make up for it though,' answered Mr MacDonald. 'People start going away for a few days' holiday this time of year.'

'We're going away soon,' interrupted Sarah. 'Won't it be fun? We'll be off first thing in the morning.'

'Not first thing,' corrected Mr MacDonald. 'If we go in the middle of the morning we'll miss the worst of the traffic. It will be a much more pleasant trip then.'

'I like it when we don't have to go to school,' exclaimed Paul. 'The best thing about school are the times when you don't have to go.'

'You rascal!' said Mr MacDonald. 'You don't really mean that. In spite of all the fuss you make about school, you enjoy it most of the time.'

'Let's change the subject,' suggested Mrs MacDonald. 'What did Mr Hill preach about this morning?'

'The Holy Spirit.'

'Yes, but what did he tell us about the Holy Spirit.'

Sarah answered first. 'He said the Holy Spirit is the gift of God the Father and the Lord Jesus to all Christians.'

'That's right,' replied Mr MacDonald. 'Anything else, Paul?'

'God the Father and the Lord Jesus sent Him because They had promised to do so.'

Sarah nodded her head in agreement. 'He was sent to stay with Christians forever. He'll never leave them. Right up to the time Christians die, He stays with them.'

'Yes,' added Paul, 'and He was sent so that He might live in Christians. We can't see Him living in us, but He does if we trust in the Lord

16

Jesus.'

Mrs MacDonald was pleased to see how much the twins remembered of what Mr Hill had said. 'Just as this house is your home,' she explained, 'the Holy Spirit wants to make our lives His home.'

Sarah looked puzzled.

'What's worrying you, Sarah?' asked Mr MacDonald.

'Well, sometimes you and Mum talk about the Lord Jesus living in us when we trust Him. And then sometimes you talk about the Holy Spirit living in us. My Sunday School teacher does the same. Do they both live in us? Or does just one?'

'Let me ask you a question first,' replied Mr MacDonald. 'There is God the Father. There is God the Son. And there is God the Holy Spirit. Does that mean three Gods?'

'Of course not, Dad!' replied Sarah. 'You have explained that before.'

'Good,' answered Mr MacDonald. 'There is only one God. What we say of one Person of the Trinity we may say of each Person. If we are Christians, we can say that God the Father lives in us. Or we can say the Lord Jesus lives in us. Or we can say the Holy Spirit lives in us.'

17

'Yes,' interrupted Paul, 'but God the Father and the Lord Jesus are in heaven, aren't they?'

Mr MacDonald agreed. 'We know that God the Father and the Lord Jesus are in heaven and that it's the Holy Spirit who's here on earth. It's the Holy Spirit, therefore, who lives in Christians. But the Holy Spirit, the Lord Jesus and the Father are so much one that it's really the Father and the Lord Jesus living in us too.'

Sarah was pleased that she understood more now about the Holy Spirit's living in a Christian.

Paul had a question. 'When we trust in the Lord Jesus and the Holy Spirit lives in us, what is He there for? What does He do in us?'

'That's like asking what's the use of the air that we breathe, Paul!' said Mr MacDonald. 'We can't live without air and we can't live as God wants us to live without the Holy Spirit's help.'

'How does He help us then?'

'First of all, He helps us to understand what it means to be a Christian. Most people are confused about this to start with. Sometimes they think that being a Christian is going to

18

church.'

'But Christians do go to church, don't they, Dad?' said Paul.

'Yes, but it isn't just going to church that makes you a Christian, is it?'

'No,' replied Paul, 'it's really believing in the Lord Jesus and trusting Him as Saviour.'

Mr MacDonald continued, 'Perhaps some people think that it's only a matter of trying to do their best and helping others that makes people Christians. But the Holy Spirit speaks to us through the Bible, when we hear it taught and preached. He shows us that being a Christian is turning from our sin and then trusting and obeying the Lord Jesus. Suddenly, perhaps, a person feels that God is speaking just to him or her and no one else.'

'I understand that,' said Paul. 'At the special Youth Service at church I felt just like that. When the speaker told us about the two kingdoms - Satan's and God's - I knew what he meant. I saw that I could become a member of God's kingdom only by trusting in the Lord Jesus.'

'You knew that before then though, didn't you, Paul?' enquired Mrs MacDonald.

Paul agreed. 'Yes, I'd known it a long time.

But I felt then that God was really speaking to me. I knew that I ought to ask God to forgive my sins, although I still didn't do anything about it.'

Mr MacDonald nodded, for he understood. 'I'm sure that it was the Holy Spirit who was speaking to you then, even though you didn't fully respond. He's helping you to understand what the Bible teaches us about being a Christian. And He will keep on doing so. Once we've become Christians, He wants us to be like the Lord Jesus most of all. Sometimes He will make our conscience worry us when we've done something wrong or haven't done something we should have done. Do you remember that man who came and asked me for money for food when we were away last year?'

'Do you mean the man who looked rather dirty, and whose clothes weren't very clean?'

'Yes, I remember,' said Sarah. 'When Paul and I stared at him, Mum told us not to be rude. Then after we had all walked on, you went back and gave him some money.'

'You've a good memory,' said Mr MacDonald with a smile. 'When he first came up to me I thought, "He looks hungry." Then I thought, he must be lazy and doesn't deserve

20

to be helped. But as we walked on, my conscience made me feel uncomfortable. I thought, Jesus would have helped him. I knew then that I must go back and give him some money to buy a meal. I think it was the Holy Spirit helping me to see what I should do. It's so easy to be selfish, but the Holy Spirit won't let us stay like that.'

Mr MacDonald looked across the table to Mrs MacDonald. 'Is there anything I've forgotten?' he asked.

'You haven't mentioned how the Holy Spirit helps us to understand the Bible and also to pray,' she suggested.

'Thank you. Yes, the Holy Spirit helps us to understand the Bible as we read it. He's the best person to do this because He helped the people who wrote the books of the Bible. Every time we read the Bible it's important to ask the Holy Spirit to help us to understand it.'

'Do you always do that, Dad?' Paul asked.

'Sometimes I forget, but I try to remember each time I read the Bible how much I need His help.'

'And what about prayer?' Sarah asked.

'He also helps us to pray,' continued Mr MacDonald, 'especially if we ask Him to do so.

And there's another thing,' he added. 'He makes us strong and courageous to serve God. Do you remember learning about the apostle Peter saying he didn't know the Lord Jesus?'

'You mean in front of the servant girl in the high priest's palace, Dad?'

'That's right, Sarah. What made the difference on the day of Pentecost when Peter spoke so bravely to thousands of people all at once about the Lord Jesus?'

'The Holy Spirit,' suggested Paul.

His father nodded. 'And whenever we serve God, it's the Holy Spirit who helps us so that we're not afraid.'

Mrs MacDonald looked at the clock. 'Time to clear the table, everybody.'

'One more question, please,' said Sarah.

'All right.'

'How do you know if the Holy Spirit is in you?'

Mr MacDonald smiled. 'How do you know that you're alive, Sarah?'

She thought a moment. 'Well, I was born. I've just eaten my dinner. And I do lots of things which show I'm alive.'

'You've helped to answer your question then,' explained her father. 'If you've been born into God's family by receiving the Lord Jesus into your life as your Lord and Saviour, you've received the Holy Spirit. And if you find you're hungry for the Bible...'

'What do you mean by being hungry for the Bible?' Sarah interrupted.

'I mean that you want to read it and obey it. And if at the same time your life becomes more and more like that of the Lord Jesus, then you may be sure that the Holy Spirit lives in you.'

'Any volunteers for doing the dishes?' asked Mrs MacDonald.

'You and you,' said Mr MacDonald, pointing at Paul and Sarah with a laugh, as he helped to stack the plates and dishes.

3   An Early Start

The MacDonalds were up early on Monday morning.   As usual, the twins were awake before their parents and they had difficulty in keeping quiet because of their excitement. At half past six they crept down the stairs to make their parents' early morning cup of coffee. They knew this would be a good excuse for waking them up!

Sarah tried to carry the cups up on the tray without spilling any coffee in the saucers but without success.

'You're an old wobbler!' teased Paul.

'I can't help it,' replied Sarah.   'I try my hardest.'

'What's all the noise?' asked their father from the bedroom.   'Get back in bed and go to sleep.'

'It's quarter to seven, Dad,' shouted Paul.

'Yes, and we have made you a cup of coffee,' added Sarah.

'That's all right then, isn't it, Dad?' Mrs MacDonald suggested from the bedroom.

'I think it's bribery,' commented Mr MacDonald.

'Bring it in, please,' Mrs MacDonald

added, 'and in a few minutes I'll come down and start getting breakfast.'

Sarah carefully poured the coffee from the saucers back into the cups.

'Old wobbler has carried the coffee up this morning,' explained Paul.

'Don't tease, Paul,' said his mother.

* * *

As soon as the breakfast dishes were cleared away, Paul and Sarah started bringing downstairs the things they wanted to take away with them.

'What time are we leaving?' Sarah asked her mother.

'When we're ready!' replied Mrs MacDonald, who was busy in the kitchen. We can't leave everything untidy for Grandma and Grand-dad.'

At that moment Paul came out of his bedroom and ran straight into his father who was carrying a suitcase down the stairs.

'Watch where you're going, please, Paul.'

'Sorry, Dad. I want to get another game in case it rains while we're away and we have to stay indoors.'

Mr MacDonald looked at the piles of games and books that Paul had stacked in the

hall, and he groaned. 'We can't take all of those things. It's a truck we'll need, not a car! We're not moving house, you know. We're just going away for a few days!'

Mrs MacDonald heard the conversation, so she said, 'Two books each and two games each. That's all. And no more getting in the way, running up and down the stairs. Please go and sit in the front room and read until everything's in the car. I won't be long now.'

Rather reluctantly Paul and Sarah did as they were told. Paul had his father's guidebook and the twins were soon making plans for the holidays. Time passed so quickly that it wasn't long before they were in the car, and their journey had begun.

* * *

'We're still looking for place names beginning with the letters of the alphabet,' Sarah explained.

'What letter are you up to?'

'H,' replied Sarah. 'We've been looking for a sign with that letter for ages. I hope we see one today.'

When they were about halfway there, the twins still hadn't seen an H. They decided they would play another game if they didn't see one soon. As they had been travelling for about an hour and a half, Mr MacDonald suggested stopping for a snack at the next pleasant spot they came to.

They saw a sign to a park and followed its directions. It was at the top of a hill giving a beautiful view of the surrounding country. Paul and Sarah really felt that they were on holiday now.

'What were you both talking about and looking at when we were packing things into the car?' Mrs MacDonald asked the twins.

'Dad's guidebook,' replied Sarah.

'And it says that there's an old church close to where we'll be staying, which was one of the first in that part of the country.'

As Sarah listened to what Paul said, a question came to her mind. 'When was the first church, Dad?'

'Do you mean the first church building in our country?'

'No, the first anywhere.'

'That's rather difficult to answer,' her father explained. 'The first Christians were Jews living or visiting in Jerusalem. They used to meet together in the temple if they lived in Jerusalem or in a synagogue elsewhere.'

28

'What's a synagogue, Dad?' Paul asked.

'It's the name of the building where Jews meet to worship God. Later on the Christians couldn't do this because they were forced to leave the temple and the synagogues.'

'Why was that?'

'Because many Jews refused to believe that Jesus is the Messiah - the person they had been looking for ever since the Old Testament first promised He would come.'

'Where then did the Christians meet?' asked Sarah.

'Oh, they met in one another's homes. Some of the early Christians had large homes. Many of them didn't, of course, because they were slaves who lived in their master's houses.'

'Did the slaves and masters meet together if they were Christians?' asked Paul.

'Yes, that's one of the wonderful things about the Christian church. When people trust in the Lord Jesus, they learn to love one another as brothers and sisters, whether they are rich or poor.'

Paul remembered boys and girls who went to his school whose skin was a different colour from his own. 'It doesn't matter about the colour of their skin either, does it?' he asked.

29

'You're right, Paul,' agreed Mr MacDonald. 'I'm afraid sometimes people are unkind to people whose colour is different from their own. Christians should never be unkind in that or any other way. The Lord Jesus loves us all the same, whether we've yellow, brown, black or white skin and He wants us to love everyone as well.'

Sarah liked the thought of masters and slaves all meeting together in a home to worship God. 'They must have been crowded sometimes.'

'Yes, and that's why later on Christians had to erect special buildings. Remember though that the church isn't a building.'

Paul looked puzzled. 'What do you mean, Dad?'

'Well, we often call the place where Christians meet a church, but a church is much more than a building. It's a group of people who love the Lord Jesus and who regularly meet together to worship and serve Him.'

'When did the church begin, Dad?' asked Sarah.

'The day of Pentecost was the church's birthday. When the Holy Spirit came down on the apostles, they preached the good news about the Lord Jesus.   Lots of people believed in Him and became Christians and they were the beginning of the church.'

'Time we moved on, Dad,' interrupted Mrs MacDonald.

'Let's keep on looking for letters of the alphabet,' suggested Paul, 'but let's do something else as well.'

'Such as?' asked Sarah.

'Let's see who is first to spot a tractor.'

'All right.'

4 Finding the Old Church

The MacDonalds arrived at the cottage just before it began to get dark. Grandma and Grand-dad had left it all very tidy. There was a note from Grandma on the kitchen table. Paul spotted it at once.

'Look, Mum,' he cried. 'Grandma has left a note. She says that she has put a surprise for Sarah and me in our bedrooms.'

'Good old Grandma! She never forgets you, does she? Up you go straightaway then and see what she's left you.'

Sarah and Paul rushed into their bedrooms as fast as they could and they each found on their bed a gift-wrapped parcel. Sarah managed to get hers open first. Inside she found a 500 piece jig-saw puzzle. By the time she had told Paul what was in hers, he had opened his. His parcel contained a 550 piece jig-saw puzzle. There was another parcel in Sarah's room with both their names on it.

'You unwrap it, Sarah,' Paul suggested.

Inside was the game of Junior Trivial Pursuit.

'Aren't the presents great?' Sarah exclaimed.

'Yes,' agreed Paul. 'Look, there's a note here from Grandma.'

'Oh, yes,' said Sarah. 'It says, "Please share the jig-saws and the game with one another."'

Mr MacDonald had been carrying in the heavy suitcases and had heard the twins talking about their presents.

'Grandma knows you two very well!' he said laughingly. 'She knew she ought to tell you to share these presents so that you wouldn't squabble.'

'We won't squabble, Dad,' replied Paul.

'Let me look at your jig-saw puzzle, please,' Sarah asked Paul.

'Oh, no,' answered Paul, 'not until I've done it first.'

'You're horrid sometimes,' Sarah said.

'I thought you weren't going to squabble, Paul,' interrupted Mr MacDonald. 'I suggest you put all these new things away until after we've eaten. Then perhaps we can all play a game together.'

* * *

The weather the next day was beautiful. The sky was blue and it looked as if it was going to be warm all day. The twins went out with their father after breakfast to buy a newspaper.

'Where would you like to go today?' asked Mr MacDonald. 'We could go down to the beach, if you like. The weather is certainly good enough. Alternatively we could go for a drive in the country.'

'May we go to that old church we read about in your guidebook, Dad?' asked Sarah. 'The one we told you about in the car.'

'Yes, please,' added Paul.

Mr MacDonald smiled. 'The old church it is then,' he replied. 'How do we get there?'

Paul and Sarah had the answer all prepared. They had studied the guidebook and a road map carefully and had written down the numbers of the roads they should follow. By the time they arrived back at the cottage, their mother had cleared the breakfast dishes and so they were ready to go.

'We're off on a mystery trip,' Mr MacDonald explained to his wife as they all set off in the car.

'I can guess where,' replied Mrs MacDonald. 'We're going to find that church, I expect. I knew the twins wouldn't forget your promise to them.'

Paul hadn't reminded Sarah to keep a lookout for place names beginning with the

34

letters of the alphabet as he wanted to get the next one before her. But Sarah hadn't forgotten and suddenly she cried, 'There's one!'

'Pardon?' asked her mother, in surprise.

'A place beginning with the letter L,' answered Sarah.

'Wish I'd seen it first,' said Paul. 'We're looking for a letter M now.'

Mr MacDonald knew they were getting near the church. 'Let's keep our eyes open for the signpost to the town where the church is.'

Within a few minutes they saw the sign and shortly thereafter they were there. In the centre of the town was the church. They parked the car near its side entrance and walked into the churchyard.

'Look at that old steeple with the bell in it,' shouted Sarah.

'I'd love to ring that bell,' Paul exclaimed.

The churchyard was beautifully kept. As the Macdonalds went into the church, they talked about the time people must have spent planting the shrubs and trees.

'Here's the hymnbook they use, Dad,' Sarah said, as she picked up one from a pew. 'It isn't the same as we use at church.'

'There are lots of different hymnbooks,'

her father explained. 'Where's Paul gone?'

'I'm up here, Dad,' answered Paul. 'I've always wondered what it's like to be in a pulpit!'

'I think you should come down from there,' suggested Mrs MacDonald. 'We mustn't make anything untidy. Everything is wonderfully polished and cared for.'

'Yes,' added Sarah, 'you can smell the polish - just like when you've been polishing the furniture at home.'

Mr MacDonald nodded in agreement. 'The people who are members of this church,' he said, 'must love it very much and work hard to keep it so nice.'

'I wonder how many members there are?' Paul said. 'How do you become a church member, Dad?'

'What do you mean?' asked Mr MacDonald. 'Do you mean a church like this or do you mean a member of the church of the Lord Jesus in every part of the world?'

'Both, I think,' said Paul.

'Well, there are different ways of becoming members of the many churches you find everywhere. To belong to some churches you have to be baptised and confirmed. Then at baptism children have the sign of a cross made

37

on their forehead with water as a kind of promise that when they are older they won't be ashamed to confess their faith in the Lord Jesus. But, of course, this usually takes place when children are very young and they won't know what's happening. And so at confirmation, they make these promises again for themselves and promise to be faithful to the Lord Jesus to the end of their lives.'

'Wasn't that what happened when we visited Aunt Joan and Uncle John to see their new baby daughter and when we went to church with them on the Sunday morning?'

'Yes,' nodded Mr MacDonald. 'In some other churches you become a member by being baptised when you're older - perhaps at about the time you might be confirmed in a church like this. In other churches you become a member by asking to join the church. The minister welcomes you, by shaking your hand on behalf of all the church members, at a communion service.'

Paul remembered what his father had said when he had first asked his question. 'What did you mean, Dad, when you spoke about being members of the church of the Lord Jesus in every part of the world?'

'I'll try to explain,' Mr MacDonald said. 'Every group of Christians meeting together is only a small part of God's true church which is to be found throughout the world. You could be called a member of a church like this, or any other church, without really being a member of God's true church. It's very important to belong to God's church, which is made up of His children everywhere.'

'How do you belong to that church then?' Sarah asked thoughtfully.

'By having faith in the Lord Jesus, Sarah,' answered Mr MacDonald. 'Our faith in the Lord Jesus must be a real and living faith if we're to belong to His church.'

'What do you mean, Dad?' asked Paul. 'I don't really understand.'

Mr MacDonald nodded. 'Think of two boys. The name of one is Stephen and the name of the other John. You tell me which has a living faith if I tell you what they can truthfully say about the Lord Jesus. Stephen says, "I believe that Jesus lived here on earth and died on the cross." John says, "I believe that Jesus lived here on earth and died for me on the cross. I've asked Him to be my Saviour." Which boy has the living faith, do you think?'

'John,' answered Paul.

'That's right,' agreed Mr MacDonald. 'Think of it another way if you like. Here's my set of keys. Only one of them fits the front door of Grandma and Grand-dad's cottage. Now the only key which opens the door of God's church is faith in the Lord Jesus. The key of trying our best or being a church member won't open the door. Only the key of trusting in the Lord Jesus will do.'

'I think I understand,' said Paul. 'When you ask the Lord Jesus to become your Saviour and you believe in Him, you then belong to His church with its members all over the world.'

'Yes, that's right.'

'Well,' asked Paul, 'if you belong to the church of Jesus everywhere, why do you have to belong to a church like this one as well?'

Mr and Mrs MacDonald laughed. 'That's a good question, Paul,' answered Mrs Macdonald. 'I think you'd better let Dad answer that later on. Your cousin Mark joined his church last week. Perhaps Dad will explain to you why.'

'Can we buy a picture postcard of the church if a shop sells them in the village?' Sarah asked.

'Perhaps the shop will sell ice cream cones too,' added Paul.

'No doubt,' said Mr MacDonald with a laugh.

5 Questions at Bedtime

As far as Paul and Sarah were concerned, the first day at the cottage had been great, especially the visit to the old church. Sarah had bought a picture postcard of the church. She didn't want to send it to anyone because she wanted to take it home to show her school friends where she had been.

They spent the afternoon on the beach. The sun was very warm and the water wasn't too cold. The hours just seemed to fly by and the afternoon passed in no time.

Sarah and Paul arrived back at the cottage rather hot and sticky.

'Do you know,' exclaimed Mrs MacDonald in surprise as she looked at her watch, 'I didn't know it was so late. I thought I'd do something special for our evening meal today, as we had only sandwiches at lunch time.'

'How long will it take to cook it?' asked Mr MacDonald.

'I'll need about an hour.'

'I've a suggestion, twins. You two must have a bath this evening to get rid of all that sand. You shouldn't have a bath soon after a large meal, so I suggest you both have it quickly now, so that you're ready for bed before we eat. We're not expecting any visitors here.'

'Eat in our pyjamas!' cried Paul.

'Yes, it won't matter for once.'

'Can we play some games afterwards then?' asked Sarah.

'All right. I'll play a game with the first person to have a bath and be ready for bed!'

Paul and Sarah rushed to the bathroom as fast as they could.

'I've never seen you two so eager for a bath!' Mrs MacDonald commented laughingly. 'Ladies first, Paul. While Sarah has her bath, you play a game with Dad. That will be fair.'

* * *

Sarah and Paul were quite clever at making excuses for staying up late. At eight o'clock they were still playing Trivial Pursuit.

'Our cousin - Mark - is good at Trivial Pursuit, isn't he, Paul?'

'Yes, but he's much older than we are.'

'Did you say he became a member of his church last Sunday, Dad?'

'That's right, Sarah. I wrote to tell him how pleased Mum and I are about it.'

Paul broke in. 'Will you answer my question now then, please, Dad? I mean the

one about why you have to belong to a church.'

His father smiled. Paul probably thought he could stay up later by asking questions.

Mrs MacDonald knew what her husband was thinking and she said, 'I did suggest you would tell him. They can stay up a little longer as we're on holiday.'

'Well,' began Mr MacDonald, 'Mark's a Christian. He put his trust in the Lord Jesus when he was away at a camp last summer. There have been lots of little things that have shown that he really intends to serve the Lord Jesus. One of them is that he wants to belong to the church he goes to.'

'Yes, but why?' asked Paul. 'You can still go to a church without being a member of it, can't you?'

'First of all, Mark has joined his church because he knows that a Christian can't live the Christian life on his own. The Bible uses pictures - not drawings but word pictures - to tell us what the church is like. All of these pictures remind us that Christians need one another.'

'What kind of pictures, Dad?' asked Sarah.

'It describes the church as a flock, a building, a body and a family - to mention just some.'

Mrs MacDonald joined in. 'Let me try to help you understand. Can you have a building made of one brick?'

'No.'

'Can you have a flock with just one sheep?'

'Of course not.'

'Is an ear any use without the rest of the body?'

'No!'

'Can you have a family with just one person?'

'No!'

'Good,' Mrs MacDonald went on. 'When the Bible describes the church as a flock, a building, a body and a family, it's telling us that a Christian isn't meant to live the Christian life on his or her own. He or she is to live it with the help of others.'

'I think I understand that,' nodded Paul. 'But why does God want Christians to join a church?'

'That's easy,' replied Mrs MacDonald. 'There are things God wants Christians to do together. He's pleased when Christians meet together to praise Him by singing psalms, hymns and songs. Christians can, of course, sing these on their own, but God is especially pleased when they do so together. The same is true of prayer. God hears us when we pray to Him on our own. But He's glad when Christians pray together. And then there are certain things God has told us to do - like baptism and the communion service.'

'Tell us more about baptism, please,' asked Sarah. 'And what happens at a communion service?'

'Those subjects will have to wait for another evening - or perhaps two evenings!' exclaimed Mr MacDonald. 'But Christians join together for these things. And, of course, they serve God together. It may be by teaching in the Sunday School, or by visiting people around the church and trying to tell them about the Lord Jesus. All these things Christians do through belonging to a local church. God wants a Christian to find work to do with other Christians. Could you play a game of football just by yourself, Paul?'

'Of course not.'

'Does everyone play in the same position?'

'No, there are different positions for each person.'

'But is everyone important in the team?'

47

'Oh, yes,' exclaimed Paul.

'The same is true in a church. In a church you have many people and each one has a job to do which pleases God and which will help others. One man may be able to preach and so he preaches to help others understand God's Word.'

'That's like Mr Hill at our church, isn't it?' asked Paul.

'Yes,' nodded Mr MacDonald. 'Some are able to teach God's Word, and so they teach it in the Sunday School.'

'That's like Miss Leonard and Mr Eaton, our Sunday School teachers,' suggested Sarah.

'Others are good at doing things with their hands and so they help look after the church buildings,' continued Mr MacDonald.

'You sometimes help decorate rooms at church, don't you, Dad? And Mum and some of her friends made new curtains for the church office and one of the committee rooms.'

'Yes, Paul. It's great fun doing those things together, and especially to know that it's something special you can do.'

'Are there any other jobs people can do in the church?' asked Sarah.

'Oh, lots and lots! I can't think of them all.

There are people who spend a lot of their time visiting the ill and the elderly. I'm sure that their work pleases God very much.'

'What's the most important thing that goes on in a church, Dad?'

'There's no doubt about the answer to that, Paul. It's the preaching of God's Word. You see, it's through God's Word that God speaks to us. God feeds our souls by His Word. What do you think is the most important thing Mum does for us every day?'

'I know,' answered Sarah. 'It's cooking our meals and making sure we eat enough.'

'Good. Well, God puts Christians into churches, wherever they live, so they can be fed from God's Word. And whenever God sees Christians meeting together to hear His Word, He's pleased.'

'I wonder if cousin Mark knows all this,' Sarah said quietly.

Mrs MacDonald smiled. 'I'm sure he does. But you can ask him when he comes to stay with us. Time for bed now, twins.'

'Oh, no!'

'Oh, yes!'

'Can't we have just one more game, please?'

Their mother remembered they didn't have to go to school the next day. 'One game then and only one - and a short one!'

6   Sightseeing

One of the most exciting days of Paul and Sarah's holiday was when they went to see a disused light-house. They'd been looking at the guide-book, the one that had told them about the old church, and discovered that not many miles away from it was a light-house which was no longer in operation. They were excited about this discovery because they'd both read a book about a ship being saved from rocks through the beacon light of a light-house and they had seen in a museum the way a light-house works.

They arrived at the right part of the coast early in the afternoon, and soon found a signpost which read 'To the Light-house'. Mr MacDonald drove the car up a bumpy road until they were as near as possible to the light-house. As soon as they stopped, Paul and Sarah ran on ahead of their parents to see what they could find. Exploring new places was something they both enjoyed.

They had to climb up steps cut into rock to get to it. Soon they were standing at the bottom of the light-house, looking out to sea.

Paul craned his neck and peered up at the

top of the light-house. 'We'd better wait for Mum and Dad before we go inside.'

Although the light-house was no longer used because it had been replaced by an unmanned automated station further along the coast, the light-house had been carefully looked after and visitors were allowed to climb the spiral staircase inside the tower.

'There wasn't much room for the men who manned the light-house to live,' Sarah said.

'Well, at least they were on land and not stuck on one of the small island light-houses where you have to stay for several weeks at a time,' commented Paul.

'It's great here, Paul, and you can see so far out to sea from the top.'

'I wonder how many ships were saved from danger because of its light,' said Paul, thinking aloud. 'I'm going to do a drawing of it; I must make sure I get right the number of floors and windows.'

'Me too. And we can look in the guide-book and find out when it was built and when it stopped being used.'

By the time they were back in the car, it was almost time to think about making their way home. But the weather was so good that Mr

MacDonald said that they could go home a long way round to make the most of the afternoon.

'What game shall we play?' asked Paul. 'Could we look out for things?'

'All right,' agreed Mr MacDonald. 'Since we were talking about the church yesterday and churches, why don't you try to count the different kinds of churches you see?'

'Okay, Dad. That will make a change from looking out for names of places.'

As they drove along Paul and Sarah tried to look out through all the car windows to see who could spot churches first.

'Look! There's one,' shouted Paul. They couldn't yet see what the name of the church was, but it wasn't long before they drove right past it.

'It's St Paul's Church, Dad,' cried Paul. 'It's an Episcopal church, like the one near the cottage.'

'Oh, look!' exclaimed Sarah. 'There's another church on the other side of the street.' It was a Roman Catholic church.

As they went along the twins kept their eyes open to see as many churches as they could. Sarah had a pencil and paper, and she was writing down the names of the churches. The speed of the car made it hard to write clearly.

'There's another one,' shouted Sarah. 'It's a Congregational church.'

Paul and Sarah were surprised at the large number of churches they discovered. They saw a Baptist church, an Evangelical Free church, a Presbyterian church and a Salvation Army citadel.

By the time they were near home, Paul and Sarah had made quite a long list. They had seen two Evangelical Free churches, four Roman Catholic, one Greek Orthodox, one Congregational, five Baptist, three Methodist, two Presbyterian - Sarah could not spell that one very well - two Salvation Army halls, one Community church, another hall (which Mr MacDonald explained was the place where the Christian Brethren met) and an Episcopal church.

'How many churches have we seen altogether?' asked Paul. 'Let's count up. One, two, three...'

They counted and discovered that they had seen twenty-three churches on their way home.

'Wow!' exclaimed Sarah. 'What a lot of churches!'

'And you know, Dad,' added Paul, 'some of

them were almost next door to one another.'

'Yes, Dad. On one street a Methodist church was right next to a Baptist church. I should think you could get mixed up and go into the wrong church there!'

'Dad,' said Paul, 'why aren't all the churches called the same? Why do they use all these different names?'

Mr MacDonald smiled. 'That's a hard question. Really all the churches are called the same.'

'What do you mean, Dad?' asked Sarah.

'Well, they're all called churches and they would all think of themselves as Christian churches. We don't say the creed in our church at home, but we do at the church we visit when we stay at Grandma and Grand-dad's cottage. Do you remember how it begins? "I believe in God the Father Almighty..." '

Paul and Sarah nodded.

'Well, all Christians in evangelical churches would believe the creed and would be glad to say so. If you said to the people in evangelical churches, "What makes a church?" they would probably say, "A church is a group of people who love the Lord Jesus and want to serve and obey Him." The names of the churches are the result of events in our history.'

Sarah asked, 'What do the names mean then, Dad?'

'Most of the names don't show what the churches believe about the most important facts of the Christian faith. The names show how the churches are governed or some special teaching they feel to be important.'

'What do you mean by "how the churches are governed"?' asked Paul.

'Well, every church has to be governed, or kept in order, just like schools. You have to have a head or principal in a school, and perhaps an assistant head or assistant principal as well.'

'Oh, yes,' answered Sarah, 'there is an assistant head at our school. Her name is Mrs Briggs.'

'What would your school do without a head or principal?'

'I don't know,' laughed Sarah. 'Things would get out of order. They do sometimes now!'

'It's the same in the church,' explained Mr MacDonald. 'You need to have people to govern and guide the church, but often those who do so have different names in different churches and do things in different ways, just as in some schools you have a head and in others you have a principal.'

'How is the Episcopal church we go to when we are at Grandma and Grand-dad's cottage different from our church at home then, Dad?' asked Paul.

'The answer is quite simple. In the Episcopal church the people who govern the church are the bishops. But in our church at home the elders and deacons do this. They look after only one church, but a bishop looks after many churches.'

'What happens at a Presbyterian church?' Paul asked.

'A Presbyterian church is governed by elders. Another name for elders is "presbyters," and that's how you get the word Presbyterian. A Presbyterian church is kept in order by elders who guide their local church and who may also help govern a group of churches.'

'What about a Congregational church?' asked Sarah.

'All the congregation - at least the people who belong to the church - appoint their minister and deacons. No one outside the church has the right to tell them what to do.

The congregation looks after itself.'

'We haven't asked about a Baptist church yet,' reminded Paul.

'A Baptist church is really like a Congregational church in the way it's governed. But it's called a Baptist church because its members believe that only grown-ups who believe in the Lord Jesus should be baptised and not little children or babies like in the church we visit when we stay in the cottage.'

'You still haven't told us any more about baptism, Dad,' Sarah reminded her father.

'There's not time now. But your cousin Mark's coming tomorrow. He's just become a church member. Why don't you ask him about it? But there's one thing I do want you to remember and understand.'

'What's that?' enquired Paul.

'Although churches have different names, true Christians know that the most important thing about a church isn't its name but the fact that the good news of the Lord Jesus is taught and preached from the Bible. I don't much care what the name of a church is so long as it's truly loyal to the Lord Jesus. That matters most.'

'I'm looking forward to church spotting

again,' said Sarah.

'How many did we see this time?'

'Twenty-three.'

'I don't think we'll find many more than that on one day,' suggested Paul.

'I guess we'll have to wait and see!'

7   Cousin Mark's Visit

Sarah and Paul were very excited when they awoke the next morning. This was the Saturday their cousin Mark was coming to visit them. He had sent a postcard the day before to say he would be on the train arriving at 10.31.

The twins had made all sorts of plans for what they wanted to show him while he stayed with them for the weekend. Mr and Mrs MacDonald reminded them that Mark was coming to enjoy his time with them, and wasn't to be rushed off his feet here, there and everywhere. But they said this with a smile, knowing that Mark enjoyed the twins' company and was well able to keep them under control.

Sarah and Paul were determined not to be late at the station and they worried their father so much that at quarter past ten they were waiting there. It seemed a long time before the train arrived. At last lots of people came pouring through the gate. Sarah and Paul were quite sure that Mark wasn't on the train because he was nowhere among them.

Suddenly Sarah saw him. 'There he is.'

'We thought you weren't coming, Mark,' exclaimed Mr MacDonald.

'I'm afraid I nearly missed the train. I just managed to clamber into the rear of the train, so I had to walk farther than most people when the train stopped here. It's good to see you all.'

'We've lots of things to do,' said Paul excitedly.

'We're going to take you up a steep hill right away,' added Sarah.

'Hey, wait a moment,' Mr MacDonald interrupted. 'We're going home first to give Mark a cup of coffee. And then perhaps we'll go for a ride before lunch.'

* * *

About an hour later Mark was in the car again with Mr MacDonald and the twins, and they were driving as near as one could go to the top of the hill - a favourite place with the children. They went for a short walk among some of the trees, looking for wild flowers, and then climbed to the top. Mr MacDonald stayed in the car. There was a magnificent view from the top of the hill and they sat down for a moment to rest before making their way back down.

'What have you been doing since we last saw you, Mark?' asked Paul.

'I went to camp just the other month with

some of the boys from my church,' answered Mark. 'We took twenty of them altogether. I collected some photos only this morning before I caught the train - that was why I nearly missed it! Would you like to see the ones of the camp?'

'Yes, please.'

Mark produced the photographs from his pocket. They had stayed in log cabins and some of the pictures were rather amusing, showing the boys working and playing.

'I shouldn't think the boys liked cleaning their cabins, did they Mark?' asked Sarah.

'Oh, it was fun really. We had a competition each day for the cleanest and tidiest cabin. I don't expect their cabins were as clean as their rooms at home though!'

'Did all the boys come from your church?' Paul asked.

'Yes.'

'Dad was telling us that you've become a member of your church.'

'That's right. Just before I went to camp.'

Sarah went on to explain. 'We were talking to Dad about belonging to a church and about baptism. He said we ought to ask you some of our questions.'

'What do you want to ask?'

'We were wondering why Christians are baptised, Mark,' continued Sarah.

'I think the answer to that's simple,' Mark said thoughtfully. 'The Lord Jesus said He wanted all His disciples to be baptised. He set an example by being baptised Himself.'

'Yes,' interrupted Paul, 'but didn't John the Baptist say he didn't feel he ought to baptise Jesus.'

'You're right,' agreed Mark. 'John the Baptist baptised lots of Jewish people in the river Jordan. One day the Lord Jesus came from Galilee to be baptised. But John tried to stop Him because he knew that the Lord Jesus hadn't sinned and that baptism was a sign that people were sorry for their sins and wanted to please God. So John said to the Lord Jesus, "I shouldn't baptise You. I need You to baptise me." '

'Did the Lord Jesus baptise John?' Sarah asked.

'No. But the Lord Jesus replied, "It's right for us to meet all the law's demands, to do everything God wants us to do. So I want you to go ahead and baptise Me now." It was true that the Lord Jesus didn't need to be baptised like the other people because He had never sinned. But He wanted to set an example in everything, so that we should know what He wants us to do.'

'I remember having a lesson about Jesus' baptism at Sunday school,' added Paul. 'When Jesus came out of the water, didn't the sky open - or something? And didn't Jesus see God's Spirit coming down like a dove and resting on Him?'

'Yes,' continued Sarah, 'and a voice from heaven said, "You are My Son, whom I love; with You I am well pleased."'

'Yes,' agreed Mark. 'I'm quite sure that the Lord Jesus wants us to be baptised because when He was saying good-bye to the disciples after His resurrection, He told them to go and make disciples of all the nations and baptise them in the name of the Father, the Son and the Holy Spirit. So wherever the apostles and the disciples went, they told people that if they wanted to follow the Lord Jesus, they must be baptised.'

'But why is it so important, Mark?' asked Paul. 'You can follow the Lord Jesus without being baptised, can't you?'

'I suppose you could,' replied Mark.

'When I was baptised a young Chinese fellow was baptised at the same time. He put it quite well, I thought, when someone asked him why he felt it was important. He said, "A Christian who isn't baptised is like a soldier without his uniform." '

'What did he mean?' asked Paul.

'Well, do you think anyone would want to join the army without wanting to wear a uniform?'

'No, of course not. Wearing a uniform is one of the ways you can tell that someone's a soldier.'

'That's why baptism is so important,' explained Mark. 'A person can trust in the Lord Jesus and want to follow Him without being baptised, but it would be rather strange - like someone wanting to join the army, but saying, "I don't think I'll bother wearing a uniform!" '

'You ought to be proud to wear a uniform if you really want to join,' added Sarah.

'Exactly!' agreed Mark. 'If you really trust in the Lord Jesus and serve Him, you want people to know, and you're not ashamed about it. Baptism is like putting on a uniform. When you read the New Testament you soon discover that almost everyone who trusted in the Lord Jesus was baptised. Do you remember the story of the Ethiopian who was travelling home from Jerusalem?'

'I think I do,' replied Paul.

'Didn't Philip have something to do with it?'

'Yes, Sarah. God told Philip to go down the road from Jerusalem to Gaza. It was a desert road and a rather lonely journey. But Philip knew he must obey God. As he made his way though the desert, an Ethiopian came along in a chariot. He was an important member of the Ethiopian government. In fact, he was the treasurer to the queen.'

'Why had he been to Jerusalem?' Paul asked.

'He had been there to worship God because he believed in the God who had guided the Jews and had given them the Scriptures. He was sitting in his chariot, reading part of the Old Testament. God the Holy Spirit said to Philip, "Go over to the chariot and keep close to it." Then as Philip ran forward he heard the man reading something written by the prophet Isaiah, and he asked, "Do you understand what you're reading?" '

'What did the Ethiopian say?' asked Sarah.

'He replied, "How can I unless someone helps me, and explains it to me?" He invited Philip to sit down by his side. Now the passage the Ethiopian was reading was all about how the Lord Jesus died on the cross for our sins.'

'Was that Isaiah 53?' Sarah asked. 'We had to learn some of it off by heart in Sunday school.'

'Yes, that's right. When he had read the passage through aloud to Philip, the Ethiopian said, "Tell me, please, whom is Isaiah the prophet talking about? Himself or someone else?" Then Philip began reading at the part of the Bible which the Ethiopian had been reading and told him the good news about Jesus.'

'But where does baptism come in then, Mark?' Paul asked, wondering why Mark was talking about the Ethiopian.

'Well, it's clear that Philip must have told him that if he was going to show other people that he trusted in the Lord Jesus as his Saviour and become one of His disciples, he would have to be baptised.'

'How do you know?'

'The answer, Sarah, is in what happened.

As they went along the road they came to some water and the Ethiopian said. "Look! Here is some water. Is there any reason why I shouldn't be baptised now?" '

'Was there?' asked Paul.

'Philip told him that if he really believed in the Lord Jesus, there was no reason at all why he shouldn't. So the Ethiopian gave orders for the chariot to stop. Then both of them went down into the water and Philip baptised him. The Ethiopian went home, knowing now that he didn't belong to himself any more but to the Lord Jesus.'

'Is that what baptism means as well?' asked Paul. 'That you don't belong to yourself any more?'

'Yes,' nodded Mark. 'When a person's baptised, he's baptised in the name of the Lord Jesus. If a man sells a house, instead of the house being in his name - belonging to him - it passes into the name of someone else, the man who has bought it. When we're baptised in the name of the Lord Jesus, we know that because He died for us and paid the price of our salvation, we've no right to say that we belong to ourselves any more. We now belong to the Lord Jesus. We're baptised into His name so that He can do just what He wants with our life because we want to live for Him.'

Mark paused. 'Have I answered all your questions?'

'I think so, thank you,' said Paul, looking at his watch. 'It's getting late. Dad will get tired of waiting for us. And it must be nearly lunchtime.'

'We had better run,' said Mark. 'Race you!'

They were out of breath when they arrived at the car.

'Thought you were never coming,' said Mr MacDonald. 'Your mother will be after us!'

'I'm sorry, Uncle David,' explained Mark. 'But we forgot all about the time, we were so busy talking together.'

'Will you be coming with us to church tomorrow, Mark?' asked Sarah.

'Yes,' Mark answered, 'and I'm looking forward to it.'

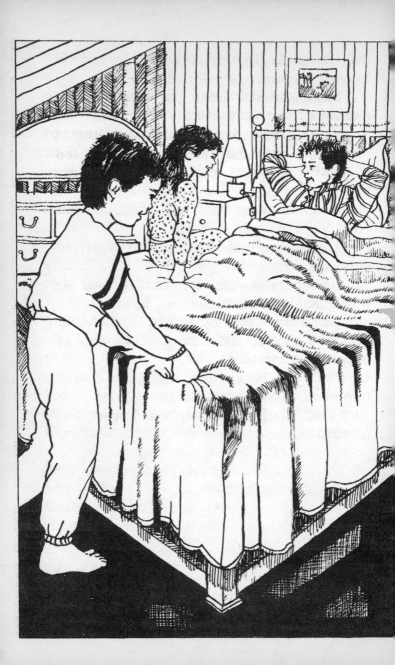

8   The Last Day

Paul and Sarah were glad of any excuse to get up early in the morning rather than have to stay quiet until it was time for their parents to wake up. With Mark in the bedroom next door they thought it was a good time to have a long talk with him all on their own. Almost as soon as it was light they crept into Mark's bedroom and found him fast asleep.

Then they went around quietly on tiptoe, one on each side of the bed and said quite loudly in his ear, 'Wake up, sleepyhead!' Mark shot up in bed with a start.

'Oh, it's you two, you rascals!' he said, rubbing his eyes. 'It's still night-time, isn't it?'

'No, it's nearly 6.30 and it's time you were awake!'

'Time I was awake!' exclaimed Mark. 'But it's Sunday today. We don't have to hurry.'

Sarah explained. 'We thought we would come and talk to you, Mark.'

Mark smiled. He didn't really mind. And so for an hour, until it was time for Paul and Sarah to get ready for breakfast they talked about all the things they had done during their time at the cottage. They were especially interested in what Mark told them about the names of some of the wild flowers they had collected. The twins hadn't known the names of some of the flowers and they had no book at the cottage to help them. They could now write the names under the flowers they had pressed in their notebooks.

* * *

Later that morning Mr and Mrs MacDonald, Mark, Paul and Sarah made the short walk to the church. They arrived there about five minutes before the service began. The organ was playing and most people were already in their seats. A steward managed to find them a pew where they could sit together. It was quite near the front.

Paul and Sarah knelt and prayed as their parents and Mark did, and then they found the right place in the prayer book where it said "Morning Prayer". Mark helped them because he was used to the book. As the service began, the twins followed it in the book carefully. When the announcements were given out, the minister of the church said, 'At the end of this service there will be a service of holy communion. We invite all who know and love the Lord Jesus Christ to stay with us and to share in this.'

Paul and Sarah wondered whether their parents would stay. When the last hymn had been sung and the blessing said Paul remembered that Mark might want to stay.

Paul whispered to Mark, 'I expect Mum and Dad will stay. Will you, Mark?'

'Yes, I will if they do,' said Mark. 'I'd like to stay.'

Sarah had an idea. 'Mum, may we sit and watch, please?'

'Is that all right?' Mrs MacDonald asked her husband.

Mr MacDonald nodded. He thought it would be good for the twins to see a communion service in a church quite different from their own.

'What page is it in the prayer book, Mark?' Paul asked in a rather loud whisper. He wanted to follow the service carefully.

'Page 45.'

Paul and Sarah were quite surprised when people left their seats and went in turn to kneel at the step in front of the communion table to receive the bread and the wine. They didn't like to ask any questions then because the church was very quiet. It was rather different from the communion service at home. There the elders and deacons passed round a plate with the bread. Then they brought the wine, and everyone drank from little glasses of wine at the same time. The twins watched and listened carefully and by the end of the service they were simply bursting with questions.

When they were outside the church again and had shaken hands with the assistant minister at the door, Paul said to Mark, 'Why did you have to go to the front?'

'Oh, this is nearly always done in Anglican or Episcopal churches,' exclaimed Mark. 'In some churches people sit in their seats, and the bread and the wine are brought to them, and in others they go to the table to receive them. But really that isn't the most important thing.'

'What's the most important thing then, Mark?'

'That we remember the Lord Jesus.'

'But don't we always remember Him?' Sarah asked. 'We remembered Him in the service this morning and the preacher talked about the Lord Jesus.'

'You're right, of course. But the Lord Jesus told His disciples that this is a special way He wanted them - and all His disciples - to

76

remember Him.'

'When did He tell them that, Mark?' asked Sarah.

'On the night Judas betrayed Him,' Mark went on to explain. 'The Lord Jesus took some bread during the supper they were having together. And when He had thanked God for the bread, He broke it in pieces and told them to eat it, remembering that His body was to be given for them. Later on in the supper, when it was more or less ended, He took the cup of wine and He told them to drink it, remembering that His blood was to be shed for them.'

'Why did Jesus want them to remember His death just like that?' asked Paul.

'I think it was because His death on the cross was the most important thing He did for us. Only by His death could our sins be forgiven and could we become God's children. We have such short memories, haven't we? By having us remember Him in this way, we're constantly reminded of His death. We can't forget about the most important event in His life.'

'Was it just ordinary bread and wine they used in church? Would they have bought the bread in a supermarket or a bakery?'

'Yes, I'm sure they did. You see, the bread and the wine are just pictures.'

'But why did Jesus say that we should eat the bread and drink the wine?' asked Paul. 'Couldn't there be a loaf on the table to remind us of His body and some wine to remind us of His blood, without having to eat or drink them?'

'We don't know the answer to that,' Mark said slowly. 'But I should think it's because eating and drinking are personal and private things.'

'I don't think I understand, Mark,' Paul replied.

'Well, what you eat and drink becomes part of you and gives you life and strength. If we want to become Christians, God's children, we must believe that the Lord Jesus died for us and receive Him into our hearts so that He becomes part of us. And that's a very personal and private thing, just like eating bread and drinking wine.'

'May I ask you another question, Mark, if you don't mind?' Sarah said.

'Yes, of course.'

Sarah continued. 'What were you thinking of when you were praying as the bread and the wine were given to you? At the communion service at home Mum and Dad bow their heads and are very quiet and still. I've wondered what they are praying about or thinking.'

'I don't know what they were thinking, of course,' answered Mark. 'But I expect they were doing what I was doing. When I took the bread and wine, I thought of the cross of the Lord Jesus and I remembered that He died for me. I thanked Him again for dying for me and I asked Him to help me not to forget it.'

'Really then, Mark,' said Sarah, 'people shouldn't take part in a communion service unless they're Christians.'

'No, they shouldn't. And that's why the minister said in the announcements that if you loved the Lord Jesus you were invited. Christians naturally wish to attend the Lord's Supper, or communion, and, when you're old enough and understand the true meaning of this, you too will want to take communion as often as you can. The early Christians did so every Sunday.'

'I'll be glad when I can take communion,' said Paul.

'Oh, I don't think it will be long now for you,' replied Mark. 'It will be good for you to have a talk with your minister at home about it and he'll explain more fully what it means and suggest the best time for you to join the church. Anyway, you're going back home tomorrow, aren't you? Next Sunday you'll be back in your own church again.'

'That's a good idea,' said Mr MacDonald as he and his wife caught up with Mark and the twins. 'But now, go and change into your jeans, and we'll take our lunch down to the beach - the last time before we go home.'

'Ugh, back to school soon,' said Paul.

'Yes,' said Sarah. 'But I'm looking forward to being back home, and seeing my friends again.'